WHAT is LAUGHTER?
MESSAGES FROM THE HEART

Lexie Brockway Potamkin
Original Art from Paintings by **ROMERO BRITTO**

Library of Congress Cataloging-in Publication Data

What Is Laughter? Messages From The Heart / [compiled by] Lexie Brockway Potamkin; Artwork by Romero Britto.

978-0-9824590-6-5 (Hardcover)

First Printing, October, 2012

Printed by Palace Press, Hong Kong.

Dedicated to Richard Scalzo,
who taught us all how to laugh at ourselves,
and to Judy Block,
who makes everyone laugh and smile.

"The most wasted of all days is one without laughter."

e. e. cummings

ACKNOWLEDGMENTS

My contribution to this book was only possible thanks to the support and love of my family and friends. I want to thank the hundreds of caring people who shared their own experiences, thoughts and joy about laughter.

Heartfelt thanks goes to my lifelong friend, Elliott Curson. Your steadfast friendship means the world to me. You are a genius.

I am extremely grateful to Juan Guerrero, my loyal friend and anchor.

To Tony Tognucci, thank you for sharing your research and wisdom. You and Sally will always remain a blessing in my life.

Thank you to Laurie Sue Brockway for your continued support, love and deep friendship.

I want to thank Romero Britto for his friendship, generosity and support. Romero's happy, inspirational art work makes this world a better, more joyful place. And thank you to Katherine Davis for your patience and coordination.

Thank you to all my friends. You are extended family and a constant reminder that success is the quality of the journey. Thank you for making me laugh and smile every day!

CONTENTS

INTRODUCTION
THE ANATOMY OF LAUGHTER

"At the height of laughter, the universe is flung into a kaleidoscope of new possibilities."

Jean Houston

Laughter is a universal language that cuts across cultural differences, global boundaries and socioeconomic status. Anyone can recognize a smile, and practically everyone partakes in laughter.

Because of its profound impact on humanity, laughter has been studied by scientists and psychologists, academics and mystics. A good laugh can make you feel better. Laughing until you cry means you've had a really great guffaw.

The people who were interviewed for this book certainly had only good things to say about laughter. All these wonderful responses led me to probe deeper into the question: "What is laughter?"

When exactly did human beings start to laugh? Is laughter something we're born with, or does it have to be learned? We've heard that laughter is the best medicine, but is it really? Is laughter peculiar to human beings, or do animals laugh? Is laughter contagious, like yawning? Has science made any serious studies of laughter? As it turns out, research on laughter reveals that it's good for you, and may even prolong your life.

Although, there are some rare and unusual conditions in which laughter can cause problems, most of us can seize the opportunity to laugh often, love more and have a full life of joy.

The Science of Laughter

Laughter actually has its own science — gelotology. It derives from the Greek words *gelos* or *geloto* meaning laugh, laughter or laughing. The discipline of gelotology studies laughter and its effects on the body from both a physiological and psychological point of view.

Sometimes these causes and effects aren't beneficial. There's a rare condition known as *aphonegelia*, where a person isn't able to laugh out loud. There are also a number of variations on what is called "pathological laughter." It's caused by various forms of damage to different regions of the brain.

Sometimes people afflicted with pathological laughter burst out laughing for no apparent reason. There are at least a dozen varieties of pathological laughter. Some of those who have forebrain damage will laugh at practically anything. This "inappropriate laughter" can cause serious social problems.

Your Brain and Laughter

Gelotology may also be considered a branch of the science of psychoneuroimmunology. This examines the effects of the mind on the body, and vice versa. As its name implies, it incorporates the disciplines of psychology, neurology, and immunology. This science recognizes the beneficial effects of laughter. Many of its researchers advocate some form of laughter therapy to treat various physical or psychological issues.

Although we have been studying laughter for some time, there remains a great deal we don't know about. For example, there's no known "laugh center" in the brain, and we don't know everything about the neural mechanisms involved in laughter. We do know that the frontal cortex of the brain activates during laughter. This produces endorphins, peptides that are released in the brain, and, like morphine, relieve pain. Scientists have demonstrated that laughter involves parts of the limbic system, which is involved in emotion.

While we inherently know that laughter is often related to humor or joy, there isn't one simple explanation or one accepted theory on why we laugh.

Sigmund Freud said laughter relieved tension and that it released nervous energy. He called it the "relief theory." This was one of the earliest theories that led us to believe that laughter is good for one's health, and that it acts as a coping mechanism when a person is upset or sad.

Humans begin to laugh between three and four months old.

Laughter isn't a learned skill or trait because babies with congenital blindness and deafness laugh. They couldn't have learned it from someone else.

Scientists have found that laughter is contagious, so contagious that it can lead to bizarre extremes. There's a case in Tanganyika in 1962. A group of schoolgirls ranging from 12 to 18 years old had a fit of laughter and crying that spread like wildfire. It went from one person to another and eventually spread to adjacent communities. The epidemic became so severe that officials eventually had to close down the schools. Amazingly, the hysteria lasted six months.

Television sitcoms capitalize on contagious laughter with the use of laugh tracks.

The laugh track was first used in 1950 on the Hank McCune Show. While the show didn't last long, television producers quickly realized how effective laugh tracks were, and started to use them.

Laugh tracks also found their way into the recording industry. The first "laugh record" was the OKeh Laughing Record in 1923. It was simply a trumpet that was intermittently interrupted by laughter. It became one of the most successful novelty records of all time, and it continues to generate sales to this day. It prompted artists as diverse as Spike Jones and Louis Armstrong to produce their own laugh records.

Since then, studies have consistently confirmed that television laugh tracks increase audience laughter and that they can achieve higher ratings for programs.

Psychologists conducted a study of the 1984 presidential debates between Ronald Reagan and Walter Mondale, during which Reagan made two humorous remarks that were followed by loud laughs from the audience. Many believed the jokes helped Reagan win the debate. To test the theory, three sets of college students were shown three different versions of the debate. Two versions included the audience reactions and one didn't. The students who saw the version without the audience's laughter gave Reagan's

performance a poor grade. Those who watched the debate with the laughter intact gave him a higher grade.

So, scientists have learned that laughter itself, completely divorced from any jokes or humorous remarks, can evoke laughter in others. This led them to theorize that human beings have neural circuits that respond to human laughter. It's as if you have a laugh detector that's coupled to a generator. When you hear laughter, you're likely to laugh.

Animals and Laughter

Laughter isn't confined to humans. The laughter mechanism is in other species.

In humans, laughter is anatomically caused by the epiglottis constricting the larynx. It's tied to our breathing, and in essence is a controlled and intermittently interrupted exhale. Animals, however, don't have a larynx or voice box, at least not in the same way that humans do, so it doesn't sound like human laughter. But when we analyze the sound spectra of what they express, we find that it has the same distinct signature of what we call laughter: short sounds repeated at regular intervals a couple of hundred milliseconds apart.

It isn't the sound that humans use in laughter that defines what laughter is; it's the patterns of notes and the space between notes that define laughter.

Interestingly, as human beings, we mostly use singular vowel sounds. Although we use different sounds, we never mix them.

You may laugh ha-ha-ha, or ho-ho-ho. But you can't do both at the same time. You can't laugh ha-ho-ha-ho. Try it!

Of course, when animals "laugh," we don't know what they are thinking or feeling, so we can't arbitrarily say their laughter is associated with joy or happiness. Research has noted a great similarity in the forms of laughter found among primates. This tells evolutionary scientists that laughter derives from a common primate species and might have been around for 16 million years.

Famed researcher Marina Davila-Ross of the University of Portsmouth in England, did a great deal of investigation into the subject. She suggests that laughter has evolved separately in each species over the last five million years. Humans have developed the form of laughter that we exhibit that is peculiar to us. She also notes that the closer any primate is to us genetically, the closer their laughter resembles ours. To Davila-Ross, this implies that primates have emotional experiences similar to ours.

Laughter and Philosophy

Laughter has been examined philosophically. John Morreall is a Doctor of Philosophy and Professor of Religious Studies at the College of William and Mary. He's also the founder of the International Society for Humor Studies.

Dr. Morreall theorizes that human laughter has biological origins as a kind of shared expression of relief at the passing of danger. In his pithy book, *The Origins of Laughter*, he proposes what he calls the Ontic-Epistemic Theory of the Comic. In essence, he

says people can't see reality as it is. We re-interpret it according to our own values, beliefs and judgments. He says that "we distort what we see in the world, adding our own cultural baggage to events and things out there." For Dr. Morreall, laughter is a response that happens when the difference between external facts and our intuitive notions and cultural concepts unravel. He claims laughter helps restore the balance.

Laughter and Communication

Neurobiologist Robert Provine's research led him to believe that laughter is a part of the universal human vocabulary. He said, "There are thousands of languages and hundreds of thousands of dialects, but everyone speaks laughter pretty much the same way."

Provine also concludes that babies have the ability to laugh long before they can speak, and that laughter is a form of communication — probably the first form of communication in the human race.

While most scientists focus on the relationship of humor to laughter, Provine believes that laughter is a social function. He found that people laugh about 30 times more when they're out socially than when they're alone.

In fact, his research showed that less than 20 percent of all laughter is a response to anything that resembles humor. People may make totally banal remarks like, "Hey look, it's John," and then start to laugh. And even when we're laughing at "humor," most of our laughter is only reserved for mildly funny things — not the greatest jokes of all time.

Laughter is more about mutual playfulness and feeling part of a group. To Provine, most research on laughter is flawed by the fact that it most often focuses on people's response to jokes. As a matter of fact, his studies showed that the speaker laughs about 45 percent more than his or her audience does.

Provine says, "Laughter is primitive and unconscious vocalization." He argues that it has a genetic component. This has been supported by research involving identical twins separated at birth or shortly thereafter. One of these examples was a study of twins he called "the giggle twins." Separated at birth, and reunited 43 years later, each of these ladies said that they had never before known anyone who laughed as much as they did — until they met each other. Provine surmises they inherited their laughter sound and pattern and their readiness to laugh — and perhaps even their taste in humor.

Provine suspects that humans may be "tuned" for laughter the same way songbirds are tuned for songs. Each family of birds has its specific family song. Certain nerve cells in a songbird's brain respond when they hear that sound. Provine suspects that humans also have specialized nerve cells that respond to laughter, and that we are also "tuned" to respond.

Laughter, he says, helps us clarify our intentions and provides an emotional context to our conversations, and is used as a signal of being part of a group. And the emotional tone of the conversation tells us something about the intentions of the speaker. It's always difficult to interpret the true meaning of a letter or an e-mail because the emotional clues we might get from the sender's tone are missing.

Laughter and Health: Is Laughter the Best Medicine?

I have to admit that this isn't always the case. There have been incidents where laughter has actually caused a heart attack or even a stroke. It isn't a great idea to laugh right after you've had abdominal surgery, or if you have broken ribs. But with those few exceptions, laughter is indeed very good medicine.

Many people are familiar with writer Norman Cousins and how he used laughter to help cure himself. Cousins suffered from various illnesses and physical problems during his lifetime, but while suffering from arthritis, he developed a recovery program that incorporated high dosages of vitamin C along with a positive attitude, hope and laughter. In his case, he watched Marx Brothers films. In his book *Anatomy of an Illness*, he wrote, "I made the joyous discovery that ten minutes of genuine belly laughter had an anesthetic effect and would give me at least two hours of pain-free sleep. When the pain-killing effect of the laughter wore off, we would switch on the motion picture projector again and not infrequently, it would lead to another pain-free interval."

Cousins' book came out in 1980, and since that time the sciences of psychoneuroimmunology and gelotology have come into being.

Current research shows that laughter does the following:

- Boosts the immune system
- Exercises the heart muscles
- Clears mucus and aids ventilation
- Lowers catecholamines
- Lowers cortisol
- Lowers growth hormone

The last three are all associated with stress.

In 2005, researchers at the University of Maryland Medical Center published a paper that reported a link between laughter and the healthy function of blood vessels. The paper shows that laughter dilates the inner lining of blood vessels (called the endothelium) and increases blood flow. Drs. Michael Miller and William Fry theorize that beta-endorphin-like compounds activate receptors on the endothelial surface to release nitric oxide, which causes the dilation of the blood vessels. Nitric oxide reduces inflammation and decreases platelet aggregation.

Many hospitals have "humor rooms" and "comedy carts." If you've ever seen the movie *Patch Adams* starring Robin Williams,

you know that hospitals routinely use clowns to bring good cheer and laughter to sick children.

Laughter and Therapy

In experiments on how stress affects the nervous system and various disease states, laughter has been shown to have many beneficial effects on health. Laughter causes changes in the autonomic nervous system (especially the sympathetic nervous system) and alters stress hormone and neurotransmitter levels.

Through gelotology, using the psychoneuroimmunology model, these forms of therapy have been established:

Humor Therapy: Also known as therapeutic humor. The technique uses humorous films, books, shows, stories and often the patients' own humorous experiences.

Laughter Therapy: Patients identify their laugh triggers, like people in their lives, things from their childhood, movies, jokes, comedians or situations that have made them laugh. Once the clinician has this information, she creates a personal humor profile. The client is taught basic exercises that they can practice. The exercises remind the patient of the importance of relationships and social support. They're huge factors in the healing process.

Laughter Meditation: Although this is somewhat similar to traditional meditation, the subject focuses on laughter in order to concentrate on the moment. It's usually a three-stage process:

- Stretching and relaxing
- Laughing or crying
- A period of meditative silence

In the first stage, the subject simply relaxes by stretching every muscle. Laughter isn't involved.

The second stage starts with a gradual smile and then slowly begins to purposely belly laugh or cry. Either might occur.

In the final stage, the patient abruptly stops laughing or crying. Then they close their eyes, breathe silently and focus their concentration on the moment. The process takes about 15 minutes.

Laughter Yoga and Laughter Clubs

Laughter Yoga is also known as Hasa Yoga. It's a form of yoga which employs self-triggered laughter. The laughter that's generated is a purely physical expression and isn't necessarily tied to any specific kind of humor or comedy. The original concept was developed by Jiten Kohi, an Indian guru. It was turned into a popular exercise routine by an Indian physician Madan Kataria, the author of *Laugh for No Reason*.

Because of the contagious nature of laughter, and the fact that we can spontaneously make ourselves laugh, it's easily stimulated in a group — especially when it's combined with eye contact, laughter exercises and playfulness. It begins with fake laughter, which quickly becomes real laughter.

Laughter Yoga brings more oxygen to the body because it's incorporated with yogic breathing exercises called pranayama. Laughter Yoga is based on the premise that the body can't tell the difference between fake laughter and real laughter; the benefits are the same, both physiologically and psychologically.

At first, Laughter Yoga was practiced in the early morning by groups in public parks. Dr. Kataria later began laughter clubs. The first club started in Mumbai in 1995. There are now approximately 7,000 laughter clubs in over 60 countries.

The primary reason Dr. Kataria called this technique Laughter Yoga was because he incorporated pranayama into the laughter exercises. The combination has a powerful effect, exerting its influence over the body, mind and emotions. Stress always changes

our breathing patterns. We know this inherently, because every time someone is upset, the first thing we tell them is "take a deep breath." Pranayama normalizes the breathing and thus our autonomic nervous system.

The word yoga comes from a Sanskrit word meaning union. In this case, the idea is to integrate body, mind and emotions. There are many paths of yoga, like Hatha Yoga, Karma Yoga, and Bhakti Yoga.

Laughter Yoga is unique because it enables you to achieve sustained hearty laughter without involving cognitive thought. It bypasses the intellectual systems that normally makes us stop laughing after a very brief time.

Laughter Yoga sessions start with gentle stretching, chanting, clapping and various forms of body movement. This helps break down inhibitions. Practitioners are taught yogic breathing to prepare the lungs for laughter. Then they are given various laughter exercises, and these are interspersed with more breathing exercises.

These sessions often conclude with laughter meditation. In this case, "laughter meditation" means that the participants sit or lie down and allow spontaneous laughter to flow naturally from within — as if they were human laughter fountains.

These sessions have many psychological and physiological benefits. Imagine if we did five minutes of laughter meditation every day before we went to work. Our day would be brighter and happier.

Reflections on Laughter

What is laughter? In this book you'll find over one hundred different definitions of laughter from people around the globe. They represent all walks of life.

They aren't the first to discuss, define and celebrate laughter. Laughter and its effects have elicited the interest of a fascinating mixture of people over time, ranging from scientists to health experts, communications experts and even yogis.

I've been blessed in my life to be surrounded by people who have made me laugh and who have shown me the power of laughter to heal and transform lives. Romero Britto epitomizes laughter and generosity. Just being in his presence uplifts your psyche and spirit. His happy, positive artwork makes you smile, laugh and feel better when you look at it. Romero is a fine artist and his loving, compassionate, giving personality is depicted in every piece he produces.

But it started with my parents. They raised my siblings and me with a daily dose of laughter and fun. It was a huge part of family life. Laughter was always served with family meals, and it was on the menu for everyday occasions.

My mother was an amazing joke teller and she constantly made me crack up. My father was naturally funny. It didn't take much for him to make me laugh. I remember a childhood filled with watching comedies together. We would sit there and howl. My Dad always called me by my nickname, "Toad." He called me Toad because I hopped around following him wherever he went. My Dad had a great sense of humor, and I always wanted to be in his presence. His loving, happy personality lifted my spirits. When I look at Romero Britto's wonderful artwork on the cover of this book, I laugh and smile and remember my nickname: Toad! Even when the family would water ski or be involved in sports, we would laugh and laugh — and laugh.

Now that both my parents are gone, I realize more than ever that they live on through memories of laughter and joy. Laughter, I believe, is often what we remember most about people and the time spent with them.

As Miss World USA in 1974, I traveled around the country with Bob Hope, the pageant's goodwill ambassador. I saw how he used laughter to truly change people's lives. And he really made me laugh! I would go on stage with him and he would ask me, how old are you? I would answer, "I am 19 years old." He would say, with a straight face, "I have golf balls older than that." From service men and women he entertained through the USO to every-day people he came in contact with, he understood how to use humor and laughter as a transformational tool.

Lexie with Bob Hope at the Bob Hope Desert Classic in Palm
Springs, California. The car alone made people laugh.

Bob was philosophical about his chosen profession. He once told me that if he could make people laugh for an hour and help them forget their troubles, then he was making a real difference in the world. He entertained thousands of armed service members, and by doing this, he gave them a reprieve from their stressful duties. He spent most of his life making people laugh.

Bob was a truly happy, funny guy, and he allowed laughter to be the foundation of his life until his very last breath. If you ever wonder if laughter truly is the best medicine, think about Bob Hope and fellow actor and comedian George Burns, who both lived to be 100.

I've come to believe that laughter truly is our birthright — a birthright we should claim and embrace. Laughter literally creates positive vibrations and can start a "good mood virus."

When I talk with people who are funny, my heart feels more open. When I'm with friends who make me laugh, I'm uplifted. When people laugh out loud around me, I want to join in. Laughter has a spiritual element; it can raise your vibration and connect you to a higher consciousness.

Our family loves to spend time with Tibetan Monks; they carry a lightness of being that is attractive and welcoming. Some of the most spiritual people I know have an uncanny sense of humor, including Rami Shapiro, Cynthia Bourgeault and the Dalai Lama.

On the special occasions in my life when I have been in the presence of the Dalai Lama, I have been again reminded what I learned from my parents, and then from Bob Hope — that laughter is a powerful form of healing and that laughing a lot is a wonderful way to live. The Dalai Lama uses his smile to reach people — and he is truly lighthearted and playful.

In his book, *My Spiritual Journey*, he explains why he laughs so frequently. "I have been confronted with many difficulties throughout the course of my life, and my country is going through a critical period. But I laugh often, and my laughter is contagious. When people ask me how I find the strength to laugh now, I reply that I am a professional laugher. Laughing is a characteristic of the Tibetans."

He adds, "My cheerfulness also comes from my family. I come from a small village, not a big city, and our way of life is more jovial. We are always amusing ourselves, teasing each other, joking. It's our habit."

My family was the same way, and to this day it's still what gets us through the tough times and rough spots. My sister and I have a special saying: "We're going to laugh our way through this life into the next one."

For me, one of the happiest sounds is children playing and laughing on a playground, or laughing in the backseat of my car while I am driving to a sports game. Children are often our greatest teachers. Laughter comes so easily to them — much easier than it does to adults.

Laughter as the foundation for living is the philosophy I use to raise my three children. They know it takes just a little bit of laughter to get you to smile more and laugh even harder. Even

when they're feeling under the weather there's a way to find humor in the situation. One day, all three were sick and feeling awful. Suddenly, one started doing an impersonation and the others danced around in a funny way. They got silly, and within the silliness, they got lighter. That night, I saw that laughter truly made them feel better!

Just as I remember the laughter shared with my parents, I hope that our legacy to our children will include laughter. I am sure they will remember the love and the spirit, but most of all, they will remember the laughter.

My husband has a favorite toast: "Here's to you, may you live to be 110 and may the last voice you hear be mine!" I've heard it hundreds of times and I still laugh.

I think we all remember the laughter in life, so let's make sure we have more of it to lighten the load and warm our days. So keep on laughing — laugh out loud, every day! Remember, time flies whether you're having fun or not.

In Love, Spirit and Laughter,

Lexie

WHAT IS LAUGHTER?

"Laughter is the ultimate expression of relief, of fun and joy. It can bring sunshine to a dark day. It lightens one's burdens. It brings valuable oxygen to your brain.

It gives your whole body some exercise to control muscle spasms. Laughter is, by all accounts, a magical, musical currency in the recreational arena.

Alan Demers, Manufacturing engineer

"Laughter to me is seeing my brother and sister play in our backyard with smiles on their faces.

Laughter is going places with my family and loving life."

Alura Potamkin, Age 12, Student

"Since we often interchange the words 'humor' and 'laughter,' I would clarify the difference between them.

For me, humor is seeing or finding something as funny. It's a mental process. Laughter, on the other hand, is the outward manifestation of seeing that funny thing. It is a physical reaction to the humorous. It's also probably wise to mention that laughter can be done without actually finding something to laugh about. That is exemplified in the recent laughter clubs — where people just laugh for no reason. It's questionable whether genuine laughter or "laugh-for-no-reason-laughter" have the same beneficial effects. But why wait for science to tell us that laughter, real or not, is good for us?

If it feels good, just do it."

Allen Klein, Author, *The Healing Power of Humor, The Courage to Laugh* and *Learning to Laugh When You Feel Like Crying*

"Laughter charms the soul and the heart with warmth and sweet enchantment. Without laughter there would be no self-efficacy. Moreover, people who have learned to laugh have redeemed themselves from the stain of an unhealthy appetite relating to anger and where loneliness abides.

In essence, laughter cheers the atmosphere from a tainted and cold environment. Respectively, laughter gives one peace and revitalizes the spirit. And most of all, laughter brings harmony, and replenishes the mind with enlightening thoughts of happiness.

In the end, laughter spreads joy and rekindles relationships that lack love."

Angela Booker, Caregiver and marketing administrator

"Laughter is like a drug. The more I giggle the bigger the infusion of happiness that seeps through my body, brain and heart.

Everything lightens up — anger softens, worries dissipate, regret melts away. Laughter puts me in a positive mindset that lets me count my wins instead of my woes; count my blessings instead of my blows; count my friends instead of my foes; count myself lucky to counteract sorrows.

I based this on a little poem I wrote for my book-and-cards set, *Affirmation Goddess, Express Your Way to Happiness.*"

Anita Revel, Author, artist and marriage celebrant

"Laughter, to me, is sudden impulse made by the emotional body to express joy. It is beneficial on so many levels. Chemically, it seems to cleanse our cells. But delving deeper, it seems to free the soul of the burden of a heavy body, if only for a split second.

Surrendering to the impulse brings about both a freedom and a direct contact to the higher self."

Barb Wilson, Food service director

"Laughter is an outward expression of joy or amusement. But it is also the heart's desire.

Laughter lifts your spirits and connects you to others in an intimate way — when you and they are less guarded and at peace.

There should be no life lived without laughter. It heals the soul and relaxes the brain."

Barbara Desy, Assistant manager, Family Dollar

"At the moment of recognition and realization, laughter can be the spontaneous acknowledgement of a truth that is profoundly felt, but indescribable.

Laughter can mean that a person feels threatened, is nervous, embarrassed or uncomfortable.

Laughter can be insensitive, haughty and even cruel.

Even very little babies laugh. They laugh when they're tickled, when they're startled, when they're excited, and they laugh at general silliness or funny faces.

My 15-year-old granddaughter says that laughter is the sound that you make when you are happy — and sometimes when you are sad."

Bhakti Ananda Goswami, Siksha Guru (Instructing Master)

"Laughter makes my heart feel good and fills my inner self with overwhelming love and warmth.

There are times when I laugh so hard for such a long period of time that I become exhausted.

Lately, I've been getting this funny feeling making me start to laugh, even over things that happened days before."

Bonnie Lennex, Delivery service

"Laughter is a way to connect with others — stranger or friend. Laughter helps me deal with difficult or awkward situations. Laughter helps me to laugh at myself and feel accepted. Laughter helps pass the shadows away."

Cara Adams, Office manager, pastor's wife

"Laughter is that unavoidable, spontaneous gurgle of humanity that starts in the belly, pours out of the mouth and lights up the face — even if it's for just a fraction of a second.

It's the joy of being with, remembering or learning about another being, another place or an idea."

Caren Browning, Public relations executive and actress

"Laughter is the physical response when something tickles my brain.

It's a great physical workout. It's an emotional release. It's a way to bond with others. Sharing laughter is like sharing a meal — a communion. When someone makes me laugh, I consider it a gift.

I am a humorist, and it is my intention to help others laugh, especially to laugh about things that are annoying or painful. If I can find what's funny about a situation, it often helps me see it differently.

To me a good hearty bout of laughter casts out despair and depression the way light casts out darkness.

Laughter sometimes is just joy. Sometimes something makes me so happy — like jumping on a trampoline with a friend — that there are no words; the only way to express my joy is to laugh.

As far back as I can remember I sang ridiculous songs, buried my nose in funny comic books and watched cartoons.

I love to laugh.

I love wordplay, being silly, telling jokes, hearing jokes.

Humor and laughter are just one coping mechanism, but of all the coping mechanisms I can think of, this is one that I don't mind if I get addicted to. I don't think it will land me in rehab. If laughter is a disease, then please don't cure me!

Laughter lightens my load."

Carla Ulbrich, Songwriter

"Laughter is the lighter spirit of my soul when it isn't bogged down with grief.

When you make me laugh you lighten my soul. It rises and it falls and it soars all over — and when it bounces back inside of me, I feel wonderful!"

Cameo Manuel, Computer lab aide

"Laughter is a path you choose.

The people who laugh most easily and with great delight have stumbled upon the notion that every life has moments of sadness and struggle. They take to laughing to brighten the dark corners in the lives of others.

They enjoy all the moments in life and embracing those that have sorrows. People who laugh a lot live deeply passionate lives. It's living large. Wherever they go, happiness goes with them."

Carol A. Chester, Catalog maintenance

"Laughter is when you forget all the agonies in life for that moment."

Bo Dietl, NYC detective — retired; movie actor/producer; private investigator

"Laughter is total joy and release of the spirit.

When my grandchildren laugh, it's totally free and exuberant. It's supreme joy in the moment. They love their experiences and interactions with people, pets and events. They open their hearts and share the moment with unabashed abandon.

I love to hear their laughter and their glee. It's contagious."

Carol Garrison, University professor

"I did my paramedic thesis on psychoneuroimmunology, or how humor heals us in many ways beyond the emotional.

Without humor to lighten up the load of living, life wouldn't be worth much. As a medic, we used humor (very dark humor) to ease the stress of the job.

Life without humor would be so dull. Laughter is a rather ethereal thing to try to define, but I wouldn't want to live without it."

Carolyn Fowler, Medical consultant

"I love the kind of laughter that follows a cry. The kind that bursts out of you with no control when your face is slick with tears."

Cheryl Bryan, Hairstylist

"You don't stop laughing because you grow old. You grow old because you stop laughing."

Michael Pritchard, Humorist

"Laughter entails a pleasurable release. People at times experience spasms of laughter that can emanate from the belly or chest and spew forth from the mouth. Afterwards, there is a tendency to smile, rest and (in men) roll over and go to sleep.

A day without laughter is like a day without music or kissing. You can do it, but life is better the other way.

Laughter is like medicine. As is romance."

Charley Wininger, Psychotherapist

"Laughter is how my husband shows he loves me. Nothing makes him happier than making me laugh.

If I'm upset, he'll listen and comfort me for a while. I can see the switch turn in his head when he decides, 'Now is the time to make Carrie laugh.' He'll do anything goofy at that point — blow raspberries on my belly, dance like a maniac or make up a ridiculous song.

All he wants is to make me laugh. He's happy when he knows I am happy."

Carrie Pitzulo, Assistant professor of history

"If only for a moment, laughter releases me from the insane notion that life is serious and difficult.

When I catch myself in a sad, sad story that's not true for me, often I find it entirely hilarious. I simply cannot stop giggling at the cartoon character I've created that I call 'me.'

My coaching clients laugh with relief when they experience breakthroughs in the thinking that has held them back.

As a member of a comedy improv troupe, I notice that audiences laugh hardest when we performers take risks and put ourselves 'out there.' It creates an intimacy which is irresistible, and a safe space for people to witness our common foibles as human beings. Our audiences respond with the laughter of recognition.

When we laugh heartily without malice, I think we are experiencing our true nature, which, minus conditioning to the contrary, is lighthearted and happy. Perhaps, then, laughter is a glimpse of enlightenment."

Carol L. Skolnick, Life coach, writer and improv performer

"Laughter is the ability to make others laugh, chuckle or even smile. I have an innate sense of comedic timing evinced in the fact that my former landlady, who trained under the writer/director Del Shores, told me so."

Daniel Judge, Performer and teacher

"Laughter is an expression of joy! It has a way of changing someone's disposition. You can be in a bad mood or depressed and the moment you laugh, it's like a drug that races through your whole being and immediately lifts your spirits.

Laughter is a true gift from God."

Deborah Seeley, Mother

"Laughter is not taking yourself too seriously. It relieves stress.

Nowadays people don't have a lot of money — but they can have fun just by finding the joy in everyday living.

God gave us laughter to be able to appreciate our faults and to be grateful for what we have spiritually within our lives.

I love to laugh. You can't buy laughter. It just comes into your life. Thank God for laughter. It's God's medicine."

Christine Ott, Retired

"It is so easy to laugh at something or someone when there is a crowd and something happens. True laughter is when I can laugh at my own mistakes and failures and see them as lessons learned.

I've learned not to take myself too seriously, I've learned to share my experiences with others. It's a true experience watching someone grow after an experience. I remember my own and my soul feels good."

Charles Maudlin, Healthcare clerk

"Laughter is an explosion of pleasure that cannot be contained. It is too big for our bodies. Irrepressible, laughter bursts forth of its own accord in joyful exclamation; a celebration of the spirit."

Donna Henes, Spiritual teacher, ritualist, author and columnist

"Laughter takes you out of the moment and provides a release of emotion. Sometimes people say, 'If I didn't laugh, I'd cry.' Laughter allows a person to move past feeling depressed and move into a more lighthearted way of looking at situations.

It's true. Laughter is the best medicine. It lowers stress levels and enhances healing. It is also infectious, as anyone who has had a fit of laughter at nothing would know.

It's an icebreaker — it's a way to bring people together, and it's fun."

Carol Wells, Registered nurse

"Laughter is forgetting the stress, sadness and hard times you may be having in your life. It's an expression of joy that one person bestows upon another.

Laughter infuses your body with happiness and tingly feelings. It can make you cry and experience difficulty breathing when the trigger of the amusement is awesomely great.

A day hasn't passed where I haven't laughed. And I don't plan to stop — whether it's a giggle, a shriek, a snort or a hearty guffaw, laughter is one of life's greatest joys."

Deborah LoSardo, Teacher

"When I first think of laughter, my mind returns to an emotionally difficult time in my life. My then-husband and I were not getting along well and the atmosphere in our home was anything but jovial.

A comment made by my daughter, who was just five at the time, hit me like the unexpected splash of ice water on one's face. Our four children and I were gathered around the kitchen counter talking about their day at school when I answered a phone call from my dearest friend and soul sister. I don't recall what she said to me. Whatever it was struck me as funny and I laughed out loud. We continued talking and laughing for a while prior to ending the call.

I then realized that all of my children had gone silent and were staring at me. When I asked what was wrong, my daughter replied, 'Mommy, you were laughing. You never, ever laugh. We thought you didn't know how.'

Needless to say, this brought tears to my eyes and an indescribable pain to my heart. I realized that I had allowed the negative energy between their father and me to affect me so significantly that I had robbed my children of knowing their mother's joy.

That moment was a turning point in my life. Since that day, 15 years ago, my life's path has had many twists and turns. Some happy, some sad. Laughter has played a significant role in each of these days.

Foremost, the lack of laughter is a reminder to me that my life has become out of balance and it's time to reflect and find my own center again. When I have done so, my day is filled with laughter. I am able to see the humor in all the quirks in life, pleasant or otherwise. It acts as a medicinal elixir, minimizing the potentially frustrating moments. It becomes a connecting thread with others as we share our sense of humor. It's a tool of humility and a reminder to not take myself too seriously. But most of all, it's a sign and indicator that I am moving within the flow of a higher power and greater purpose. It helps me to be in the 'now.'

Remembering the energy of these moments of connection helps me slow down and reflect on what is missing or what is needed when the laughter has quietly slipped away."

Carolyn Franklin, Care provider

"There is a large gulf between 'laughing with' and 'laughing at.' The former is generally good for our personal health because the kind of laughter experienced among friends is a whole-body experience in which all involved relax for a moment and share the good feeling. When we laugh at someone, we isolate that person from the group by labeling him/her as defective or less worthy.

Whoever so shames another person feels momentarily more powerful than the target of such an attack.

Whoever gratuitously laughs with others is gifted with the ability to form lasting relationships."

Donald Nathanson, Retired psychiatrist

"Laughter is just watching my daughter laugh. She makes me laugh on a daily basis. Laughter is seeing inside someone's soul."

Christine Kozanecki, Homemaker

"Laughter is truly the best medicine. When I was diagnosed with Hodgkin's lymphoma in May of 2007, I was truly scared — not knowing whether I was going to live or die.

I was a newly single parent. My ex-husband and I had been separated about a year at that point and I had custody of our two children. They were 10 and 16 at the time. It was my sense of humor and that of my family that got me through.

I remember being at a local restaurant with my entire family. We were talking about how one of my nephews was losing his hair. I said, 'Hey, watch it! Soon I'll have less hair than he does!' At first my brother and I were the only ones who laughed but then everyone started to laugh and that's when they realized that I wasn't going to give up the fight that easily. Even during my chemo sessions, I would make the other patients laugh just by sharing some stories from my childhood or talking about how losing my hair wasn't that bad because it took me so much less time to get ready in the morning.

I truly believe that if I didn't laugh about things and situations during the time of my cancer, I would not have endured the treatments as well as I did. I am cancer- free for nearly three years now and, with the Grace of God, I will stay that way for a very long time!"

Doreen Griffin-Gallway, Parish secretary

"Laughter to me, is a great stress reliever.

As for keeping the doctor away — I'm not sure about that! Anything could go wrong with your health. I laugh a lot. I have always been an easy one to get laughing. Really, it doesn't take much to get me rolling on the floor laughing. I get to the point where I need to catch a breath.

Sometimes, I find myself thinking about something funny, and my oldest child asks me, 'Mom, are you thinking of something funny again?' I don't tell anyone what I am thinking. I laugh at the weirdest times.

I have inflammatory breast cancer. Stage four. I have never heard of this type of breast cancer. So, here it goes. My opinion about laughter keeping the doctor away? Ummm, no. I don't think so!

Anything can go wrong with your health! One day you're healthy; the next it's like oh, my gosh. And not in a good way.

Yes, laughter is a really good medicine, naturally. But, it does not keep the doctor away."

Elizabeth Wheelock, Homemaker

❦

"Laughter is remembering that it is never too late to have a happy childhood."

Jeff Berkowitz, Developer, businessman

"Question: How many psychiatrists does it take to change a light bulb? Answer: One, but the light bulb has to want to change.

That is one of my favorite jokes, since it has a psychological theme consistent with my profession as a psychologist. When I tell it to people, they invariably giggle, finding it clever. I feel good making them smile. This is the power of laughter.

Laughter is the response to hearing, seeing or experiencing a comment or event that is true about life at its core but presented in an ironic or startling way. It has many dimensions. Physically, your reactions can be as scant as a smile and crinkling eyes, or as extreme as doubling over, stomach and chest contracting, emitting chortling noises and having a hard time catching your breath. Chemicals flow in the body that release stress and induce pleasure. Emotionally you feel relaxed and happier afterwards.

This is the essence of what is noted as 'the healing power of humor.' It can even be curative for diseases like cancer. As a member of the Friars Club, a famous club of entertainers and comics, I know how laughter can be a bonding experience as members get together and perform routines for each other. At the annual Friars Roast, a celebrity is subjected to the most risqué of jibes, all in the spirit of brotherhood and sisterhood. The club was founded by celebrities like Milton Berle and Frank Sinatra. Its members include Billy Crystal, Barbara Walters and Whoopi Goldberg, with Jerry Lewis as the Abbott and Freddie Roman as the Dean. A famous one-liner is from Henny Youngman, 'Take my wife, please.'

I have another personal experience proving the value of laughter to ease personal pain. *Love Phones,* my call-in advice radio show, has aired for about 10 years on music stations. We deal with people's very serious problems but we also have fun to lighten the mood. We play games such as, name five body parts in one minute. Even in the midst of recounting some tragic stories, people might say something funny that would ease the tension and relax the spirit. Further, as a couples counselor and sex therapist, I also know how humor can bond a couple going through even the most trying marital or sexual problems, and is essential to a healthy relationship.

In my book, *The Complete Idiot's Guide to a Healthy Relationship*, I encourage people to be joyful and create fun experiences in order to increase their intimacy. Also, surveys have shown that a 'sense of humor' is now among the top criteria for attraction. So in my book *The Complete Idiot's Guide to Dating*, I include lots of humorous ways and lines that can make a person positively respond to your approach.

As a psychologist, I believe that truly, as Norman Cousins famously said, there is a 'healing power of humor.'"

Dr. Judy Kuriansky, Psychologist, author, radio and TV personality

"When something funny or exciting tickles me over the edge of reason and joy I feel bubbles over to the point where I can no longer hold it inside.

Laughter is what I manifest for all to see. And hopefully join me. Laughter is much more fun when shared."

Kayama Bliss, Designer

"Laughter is the spontaneous bubbling up of joy. Energetically sexual energy and joy come from the same source. So sexual humor is particularly potent as a source of laughter if no repression gets in the way.

Laughter is a release. It releases pent up energy and it opens the conduit for joy in your being. Joy is a healing energy on many, many levels — not least is emotional. Blocked emotions zing into freedom in the presence of laughter. Laughter is best when it comes straight from the gut and explodes into being."

Eloise Gladders, Paralegal

"It opens the soul, mind, spirit and body. It also suppresses depression."

Jeffrey Washington, Technology optimization analyst

"For me, laughter is what lifts me from the doldrums of worrying about my current crisis. It connects the world in spirit and on a much lighter plane.

My life has had many challenges, and some of them have been horrendous. But continuing to seek light, joy and healing and lots of laughter with friends and loved ones has helped me.

I like to laugh at myself and with others. One of the many

funny things that happened was getting a phone call from my local car service center. My older car was in for inspection so I was a bit concerned about the message. Actually, I was told, they needed the car's registration to pass it for inspection. I thought I gave it to them—but I didn't. I gave them my voter's registration."

Hannelore Devlin, Holistic practitioner, artist

＄

"I've always been (what I consider) a funny person. Self-deprecating and out-spoken. Lately, as I age, I have come to not just enjoy laughing, but I've found it is actually a necessity.

There are times when I'm not getting on with my husband or kids and we'll watch a funny movie together, or a video clip, and we laugh together. It's very healing.

As we face financial and medical stresses in our lives we often lean on each other and watch *30 Rock* or something and laugh and laugh.

We laugh more than is called for at times because it feels good to be in that place together.

My dogs make me laugh all the time, and they respond to my laughter in a positive way."

Heather Bachelder, Church administrator

"Laughter makes my body relax. I know my situation is manageable if I can laugh.

I remember when my sister and I were sitting in a waiting room. My brother had been in a very bad accident. We just had to wait for the next two hours to go see him. Our step-sister came to see us. The three of us laughed all afternoon. She was a real comic. Somehow that laughter helped us to remember that there was a world outside that hospital waiting room and that our faces could smile again. I felt a little of myself that had shut down start to function again.

Laughter helps me remember that if I take myself too seriously I begin to think only of myself and my own ideas. I can't consider the other person's situation because I have a mission to tell the world around me all my ideas that they're obviously missing out on.

A little laughter makes my face break into a smile and raises my cheekbones. Somehow my eyes open a little differently. I relax a little and enjoy the other person. Before I know it, we are talking back and forth instead of me talking.

I relax a little more. My shoulders loosen. I see possibilities that come from everyone's viewpoints. Laughter loosens my tense body which then loosens my tense, narrow mind.

Laughter, in most situations, keeps the brain a two-way street instead of a one-way street."

Helen Jackson, Retired school teacher

"Laughter is the sound of my children when they are having fun. It's the best sound in the world.

Being a single mother and knowing that I have their unconditional love when I feel that I shouldn't is my kind of laughter. They are my own special laughter. Without them I would be nothing."

June Dobbs, Enabler

"When so much in my life is going wrong, laughter can still sneak up on me and surprise me. This is serendipitous.

Laughter can snap me away from reality when things are particularly miserable, crazy or depressing around me, or when I'm filled with sorrow.

It still amazes me how if something is funny enough I can still perceive the humor in things. When it catches me by surprise, it gives me hope that I still have some sort of connection to 'normalcy.' At times like this, I appreciate that I can still enjoy humor, whether it's slapstick, silly, hilarious or sublime.

Being able to laugh shows me I'm not that far away from happiness. I get daily jokes by e-mail. Several months ago, I was a few months behind on my rent and fighting depression. I couldn't even bring myself to open the joke e-mails. But I kept the subscription. I knew the day would come when I could laugh again.

I wasn't laughing or even smiling much in 2010. If I did, in public, much of it was forced or a facade. But I always appreciated the smallest touches of humor, especially ironic humor in the mundane, ordinary routines of daily living. I chose to just try to see my life as so ridiculous, and the things around me as so utterly nuts or ridiculous or crazy, that, like the old cliché, I had to laugh because it was better to laugh about it than cry.

And so I tried to do that. Now it takes effort, usually. But when you least expect it, and sometimes just when you need it the most, it sneaks right up and lifts you. Laughter has that power. I'm grateful for the sense of humor God has given most of us. There's a reason for it. It's a gift."

Heidi Treme, Mother, homemaker, former nurse and secretary

"Laughter is when you can take a bad situation and turn it into something that's great for the spirit.

It's when you can poke fun at how trivial things are blown out of proportion.

Laughter is fruit for the soul. I need it to get through life most of the time. In my line of work, and in my marriage, I have to maintain some sense of peace. This comes from laughter.

It's up to the individual to either laugh and have longevity, or be sad and have misery. I choose longevity.

My grandmother said that when you laugh you're defeating Satan at his game."

Jackie Jamison, LPN geriatric nurse

"Laughter is the essence of being, like bubbles of Pepsi Cola that bubble in the back of your throat and nose, bursting to get to the surface.

Laughter is the difference between throwing up on a wonderful roller coaster ride or screaming with delight at the experience.

Laughter just sings. It is the life force to living, the release valve of stress and a fountain of infectiousness that is lovingly spread to others like a living, breathing virus of the most wonderful kind. Live, laugh, enjoy!"

Jacqueline Mitchell, Psychic medium

"Laughter lightens the heart, clears the mind of dark thoughts, connects you with others and brings people together.

Laughter heals, much like tears do, but in a joyful way. A sense of humor is paramount in what I look for in a friend. One who is able to laugh at one's self, as well as life.

The best times I have with my friends and family are when we tell stories and laugh. Sometimes I laugh until I cry. It fills me with energy and bonds me to the other people I am with. It can turn around an angry or sad day.

I find a mate who can see the humor in life very attractive. I do not, however like laughter when it's used as ridicule.

Laugher lifts my heart right out of whatever pit I am in, and make me feel light as a feather."

Heather Koelle, Piano teacher, music therapist

"Laughter is like a song that is always playing and causing happiness. It's a wonderful thing to hear."

Kimberly St. Louis, Sales clerk

"Laughter is two hands that hold your soul together when times are tough, letting you know everything is going to be OK."

Jeff Falck, Photographer

"Laughter is an instant vacation.

When you tickle your child and they giggle and squeal, you light up inside and the laughter comes out in you, as well.

When you see the toothless grin of a child, that's laughter.

Laughter is something that can brighten up even the darkest of times. Laughter is the something that will never let you down.

Laughter is watching your children make a snowman and then completely destroy it as quickly as they made it and laugh during every minute of it.

Laughter is finding your best friend after years apart and realizing that nothing has changed between the two of you — and still having the same silly jokes you did when you were younger. And they still make you laugh!"

Heather Knalls, Healthcare

"Laughter is my soul's expression of joy. When laughter is authentic, it's that instinctual, guttural expression of happiness or delight.

Laughter is healing. Laughter is love. Laughter is the mask behind which we sometimes hide our pain.

Our laughter defines us — like the squeal of a teenager or the howl of a man. Before you see me, my laughter announces my arrival. It reaches a pitch that ricochets off the walls as I come closer. My laughter captures the essence of who I am."

Ju-Don Roberts, SVP, Executive editor

"Laughter is me.

I love the thought that I can be introduced to people who never smile or laugh and be the one who can make them smile and laugh.

Laughter gives me the strength to overcome the worst and to endure life's challenges.

Most of all, laughter teaches me to remain humble and to see my faults as lessons in my life and to embrace change — which is a challenge for most people.

Laughter keeps me from being sick, physically, emotionally and mentally. Laughter allows me to see others through the eyes of God so that I hate the sin but encourage the sinner.

Laughter teaches me to decipher the good from the bad; when to speak and when not to speak. Even when I'm sad, I'm laughing. When there's a death in the family I make people laugh.

I lost my younger sister seven years ago and I was asked to do the eulogy. To my surprise I had the whole mortuary laughing. I was even asked by family members if I'd do their eulogy."

Juanita F Kaisa, Chauffeur

"One can have happiness without laughter, but one cannot have laughter without happiness."

Judith R. Block, Owner & CEO of JRB Linens, Inc.

"I believe laughter is a form of protection for our sanity.

It can help make life bearable. There are times when, if I weren't laughing, I'd be crying. There are moments in my life where things are going so bad that all I could do was laugh about it.

I suppose it's a type of survival technique. Laughter is the ability where, for a moment, you can remove yourself from the harsh world around you.

Misery has no place here. I find it best to jest with others. Eventually, however, you do face reality once again, but you might feel a little bit lighter afterwards. When there is no laughter, there is no joy. Without joy, what's the point of living?

Laughter is our sanity, happiness, social connection and our strength to continue on."

Jessica Pariseau, Homemaker

"For me, laughter helps me clarify my intentions in social settings and provides an emotional context to conversations.

Laughter is used as a tool to be a part of a group — it signals acceptance and positive interactions with others. Laughter is contagious. One person can provoke laughter from others as a positive feedback, and that goes back to acceptance.

To live a long life, I must laugh on a daily basis. Hopefully, I will laugh right up to 100."

Juna Miller, Administrator

"To me, laughter is seeing a really bad toupee on someone and knowing that they think they look really good and that no one can tell.

Laughter is when your significant other is really mad and you can mimic them to get them to smile.

Laughter is the feeling you get when you realize that life isn't about the big stuff, but the small stuff that can make you happy.

Laughter is when you know what someone is thinking without even looking at them — and finishing their sentence before you both burst out laughing.

Laughter is the warm fuzzy feeling you get when you are with someone you haven't seen in a long time, yet it feels like they have always been around.

Laughter is living life to the fullest, no many how many burdens you have on your back, and can say what the heck!"

Jodi DiPietro, Bank manager

"Laughter is children, family and love. I love children because they see things so simply. They are willing to share laughter, and it's so easy to laugh with them.

Their laughter comes from the best place. The heart."

Lori Stiefermann, Children's case manager

44

"Daily laughter lets me know that I'm not taking life too seriously. It feels good not just to me but to those around me who bear witness to the joyous sound of my laughter and the accompanying emotion.

Laughter helps breaks the ice, alleviates tension and can help us consider an altered (funnier) perspective.

My mother and her siblings will often laugh at something that is rather tragic. That is, they try to find the humor in tough situations. It's probably a survival mechanism for them as they knew difficult times in their youth.

Laughter is great for the mind, body and soul. Sometimes I laugh just because someone else is laughing as they begin sharing a story. I laugh before I even know what is so funny.

Laughing is contagious."

June Soyka Cook, Self-healing website owner

"Laughter is joy to the soul.

It heals, nurtures and inspires the person laughing and the people hearing this joyous sound.

Laughter brings light that transforms the body, mind and spirit. It is a healing feeling. It is a sound that vibrates joy and freedom."

Lee Papier, Consultant

"Laughter is an emotional cure for the conscious and unconscious areas of our being.

It's an expression of who we are and how we embrace life.

I had always been full of pain and numb, so welcoming laughter into my spirit person was something I never knew how to do.

With the loving release of my negative circumstances I allowed humor and laughter to assist love, joy, peace, patience, kindness, gentleness, compassion, self-control and faithfulness, to become the person I am today."

Lana L. Incillio, Independent business owner

"Laughter is the great elixir of life. It is a healing tonic.

If you are feeling cranky or sad, there is one thing that can snap you out of it in a nanosecond: Laughter.

A good laugh alleviates tension and makes you feel good all over. We can help heal ourselves — and our friends and family — with humor and laughter. No matter how bad things get or how awful they may seem, your world can change with the simple move of your facial muscles — a slight twitch of your lips that starts as a smile and grows into a big, loud, hilarious laugh.

Even if you aren't in the mood to laugh, the act of laughing will make you laugh. I believe that laughter and a good sense of humor can get us through life's most difficult moments."

Rev. Laurie Sue Brockway, Wedding officiant, author and editor

"Laughter is the expression of sheer, undiluted joy that bubbles out and causes tears and bellyaches.

Laughter mends broken hearts. It's contagious. Hear people laughing and you'll want to join them."

Maggie Hache, Registered nurse

"Laughter is simplicity at its finest. It's living in the moment and finding passion.

You can laugh from joy, fear, love, anger or simply because of pure bliss and glee. But it truly is emotional and passionate. It is that which moves our soul.

There's no truer sound of happiness than the one of pure laughter — whether it's a giggle, a snort, a belly, a chuckle or a side-splitting laugh. You know someone is living in that moment of emotion and for whatever reason it is tickling their heart and mind's fancy."

Leila Von Steinburg Morse, Business owner

"Laughter tells me everything will be okay. It's a way of releasing tension. Somehow when things get tense or sad, humor always helps brighten things.

When I have an argument with my husband and get to a point where one of us cracks a joke, then we both know we can move on.

If I argue with someone about politics and if that person has a sense of humor, it goes over in a nice way. I use humor when I'm reprimanding my kids. They laugh instead of getting defensive."

Lisa Kelsey, Art director

"Let me first say I almost never respond to this type of query, but this one touches very close to where I live and addresses what I think is an underrated aspect of life.

Laughter is a physical manifestation of joy, fun, delight. It's what fills me up and makes the tough times bearable.

I'm sure that my husband's uncanny capacity to make me laugh — even when I am furious with him — is responsible for keeping my 41-year marriage intact.

Some families ski together, play games together and shop together. My family laughs.

I find that both the physical release and the emotional pleasure of laughter de-stresses difficult situations and gives those involved a bit of space to reconsider the stressors.

I believe that if I thought I was never going to laugh again, I would find life tiresome and depressing. But thank heavens, that is not the case."

Linda Landsman, Manages philanthropic organization, grant-maker

"Laughter is existential in life. Laughter is feeling a closeness with yourself. Laughter is funny, relaxing and intoxicating.

Laughter is life!"

Misty Harvey, Home healthcare

"Laughter is universal.

Laughter truly is the best medicine. Laughter is unbiased, non-racist, non-religious and non-judgmental.

Laughter transcends Alzheimer's. A smile can brighten any situation. Laughter makes me feel good. It can break the ice, light up the eyes and redden cheeks. Laughter is sexy and attractive.

Laughter is the best stress reliever. As my son took up skateboarding, we found ourselves in the emergency room on several occasions. My son knew I was worried about him and suddenly became the funniest person on earth. He made us both of us laugh until we cried. Through his pain and discomfort he made me laugh so much I begged him to stop or they wouldn't believe that he was really injured.

Laughter is a drug. I can carry a buzz for days with one smile from my children or grandchildren. Laughter is healing. When I went through the most difficult time of my life people were amazed that I not only got out of bed every day, but continued to make others laugh as I shared the humor I saw in my situation."

Lori Cole, Caregiver

"Laughter is energy for your soul."

Karie Lee Thayer, Driver relations coordinator, trucking industry

"Laughter is a feeling of freedom.

It can come when you are in the depths of despair. It's the ability to look at yourself and your situation and find the silly things that mean little, but help you laugh at yourself.

I laugh more with my handicapped son than I do with most people. At 26, he has the innocence of a child and the ability to say things just as he sees them, and often forces me to laugh at myself. He keeps me sane.

You can be alone and find yourself laughing out loud to a silly movie. It lets you know that you're alright.

Laughter with my sisters and brothers was slap-happy. The sillier it was, the more laughter there was. I can cry one minute with my older sister, and be laughing the next. I know we're always there for each other.

Laughter is the glue that holds the mind open for new people and experiences to come into our lives. It starts with a smile and as the relationship grows, so does the laughter.

It seems the women-to-women laughter is easier than laughter with men. It opens the innocence of the relationship. It's a healthy thing to do."

Lois Holtz, Homemaker and caretaker of an adult son with cerebral palsy

"When I was a comedian, people would ask me if I write my own material. I would say, 'No life does. I just sit by the side, with a pen and an open eye.'

Humor allows us to shift because it gives us a new perspective on our situation. We can address it with new eyes and an open heart.

Laughter is that wonderful cosmic glue that transcends race, gender, socioeconomics, culture and age. A laugh is a laugh in any language or country. It doesn't need a Berlitz guide to translate. Although that would be funny.

Laughter is the 200-watt connection that brings us back to our most vibrant, most alive self."

Lois Barth, Coach, speaker

"I tend to take the bad, negative and some of the hurtful things in my life and turn it around and make jokes about the situation. If I can laugh about it, then it can help me through that tough time.

I love to laugh and I laugh as much as I can throughout my day. I laugh with the patients that come in my office, I laugh with my co-workers. I laugh with my teenagers and my friends. I'll giggle when I'm laying in bed at night and remember something that struck me as being funny. I've giggled myself to sleep."

Lori Rhoads, Dental receptionist

"Oh, What It Is To Laugh

Without any rhyme or reason,
Nor effort or pleasing,
This delicate emotion arises from the core
Of my gentle spirit.
Discretely with subtlety, it climbs through the layers of
Hope, desperation, love, anguish, peace, anger,
Strength and weakness,
Guilt, shame, sympathy, empathy,
Exhilaration and inhibition.
It emerges brilliant and triumphant,
Glorious in its appearance.
My body welcomes the warmth, the sweetness,
Its agile way of purely being.
My heart thanks it incessantly for the simplistic joy,
Soothing away the painful scars from long ago.
My psyche remembers to mindfully capture
This precious moment in time, as if it were the last.
My soul knows no other.
The smile on my lips is offered delightfully
As if a tender gift from a child.
I naively transcend into its infinite amusement.
Please stay with me for a while.
Oh, What It Is To Laugh…"

Marie Dezelic, Writer, poet

58

"Laughter is the food that gives my soul the nutrition it needs to maintain hope.

I face so much negativity at my job on a daily basis that it drains me dry at times. When I can laugh at myself or with others, I feel like everything is going to be all right with the world — for that moment.

One of my favorite sayings is: 'Life is too short to be so damn serious.' Oh, that is so true! If more people would take the time to lighten up and be a little silly and quit worrying about what others might think, this world would be a happier place.

When I laugh I feel my body relaxing and my heart warming as the chuckle rises up from within me. There is no better feeling in the world. I look forward to laughing and I tend to be a goof just so I can laugh and possibly give others a reason to laugh with me.

Laughter can bond people. It allows them to let their guard down and be human. My kids always brag to their friends that I am a goofy lady who loves to laugh, and they love me for it. That to me is the greatest thing my kids could ever think and say about me. What a legacy."

Maria Kemp, Peer support specialist for seriously mentally Ill patients

"Laughter makes us laugh!"

Liana Brynn Pariseau, Age 5, Kindergarten student

"Laughter is a tickling in your soul, a letting go of ego and relaxing just enough to be silly.

It tells the world that something has struck a chord."

Lucille Seifer, Hospitality professional

"Laughter is a moment of release. It is freedom, heartfelt and pure."

Mark Lurtsema, Information technology

"Some excerpts from my book, *Using Humor to Maximize Living*, published by Rowman and Littlefield Education:

A universal trait is for parents to make their newborn learn to laugh and smile. Laughter is nurtured and encouraged in most of us from infancy.

Why is laughter so important? Laughter reflects the joyful side of human existence. It exemplifies hope, optimism and happiness — which are the characteristics of 'humergy,' that is, 'the energy that emerges from the joy and optimism of our inner spirit. It reflects our unique personality, and nourishes a healthy mind/body balance.'

There's a difference between humor and laughter. Laughter is a physical reaction — often to a humorous event or surprising encounter. Laughter can happen without humor and sometimes be negative or cruel in nature.

Healthy humor and laughter are actively promoted by the Association for Applied and Therapeutic Humor (www.aath.org), an organization for professionals who study, practice and promote healthy humor and laughter. The organization shares research on laughter and humor and gives members opportunities to network and support each other in their humor practice."

Mary Kay Morrison, Director, questforhumor.com

"The innocence of children's laughter is the thing that melts my heart.

A knock-knock joke told 50 times just because they were able to memorize it; their giggles as they hide under the covers and you pretend to sit on them; being tossed in the air by their daddy; tickling them until they are red in the face.

They're the best audience, and they're so easy to get laughter out of. It makes me long for that simplicity."

Melissa Blackmon, Mother

&

"Laughter is the oxygen of life. No Laughter, No Life!"

Maria Francisca Costa Azaredo, Business owner

&

"Laughter is a way to express your happiness and joy. It makes you feel wonderful. It lets others around you share your happiness and joys.

Sometimes you laugh just because someone near you is laughing. You may not know why they are laughing but you laugh along with them anyway. Why? Who knows. We just know laughing makes the world around us a brighter and happier place. I think laughter is the best medicine."

Michael Scroggins, Laborer

"Laughter is when you hear a baby laugh, it's the most amazing thing."

Ayla Potamkin, Age 12, Student

"Laughter is one of the three great releases (sexual satisfaction and tears are the other two).

If you don't get all of them on a regular basis you become stagnant. If you can get them in combination then it's exponentially better. If you're getting all three on a relatively regular basis, then energy is flowing through you and you will continue to grow."

Monica Serrato, Unemployed right now

"Laughter to me is hearing my five children talking and laughing with one another. They range in age from five to 20. The things they come up with are so ridiculous and so amusing.

Sometimes I laugh so hard that I cry."

Michelle Burris Mercado, Mother

"Laughter is a small whiff of God's breath."

Mike Piazza, Major league baseball player, retired

"Laughter is a spontaneous physical and mental response to amusement, delight and merriment. It unites every part of a person: mind, body, spirit, and senses, as well as memory and cognition.

Laughter takes me out of myself and removes me from my worries, my problems, and my aggravations. When I laugh, I'm not reliving the past or imagining the future. I'm right there in the present — with a huge smile on my face and my body convulsing in a healthy way. Laughter makes me happier and more optimistic.

A day with laughter means that my troubles can be borne a little easier and my hopes can be held a little stronger. When I laugh, I thoroughly enjoy being alive. I love to laugh."

Nikki Fiske, Third-grade teacher

"Laughter is a simple, spontaneous outburst of joy."

Julie Pearce, Owner, cleaning service

"This is too important to be taken seriously."

H. Wesley Balk, Former artistic director, Minneapolis Opera

"I think laughter is the ability to look at the world in a funny and humorous manner. People with a good sense of humor know how rough life can be and try to use humor to remove that edge.

I truly believe laughter is the best medicine because of the endorphins that are released when laughing heartily. It does make a person feel better, and it can definitely help to diffuse an awkward and uncomfortable situation.

Growing up in New York I surrounded myself with friends who also were blessed with a good sense of humor. Their jokes and sarcastic remarks were our way of maintaining those friendships which have endured to this day.

I feel sorry for people who hardly ever or never laugh because they are missing out on so much. Laughter makes one feel good about themselves. I truly believe it can considerably prolong life.

Laughter makes a person look younger, act younger and helps maintain a healthier lifestyle, in my opinion. Without laughter in our lives we are destined for sadness, bitterness, regret and sorrow — with the longing for what could have been had laughter been part of their life."

Norman Shere, Occupational therapy assistant

"Laughter is your invitation to the world to join in on your blessings, your love, your appreciation for Life."

Margie Lopez, Administrator

"Laughter is like a breath of fresh air on a stagnant day.

Laughter is liberating and makes the captive free. Laughter is like sunshine peeking through the rain clouds.

Laughter can bring tears to your eyes.

The joy that laughter brings is sometimes indescribable. Laughter eases the pain of grief. Laughter brings us closer together. Laughter keeps depression at bay. Laughter can sound like a song in a child. The happiness that laughter brings is truly worthwhile."

Patricia Baker, Educational consultant

"Laughter is that emotional release of love and enjoyment when your children play and say things that are way beyond their years.

It's the wellspring of the giggles that comes when you see something funny or watch someone act foolish just to break the tension of the moment.

Laughter is that physical expression of being entertained by a moment, person or circumstance."

Pamela Reynolds, Artist

"Laughter is the emotional Band-Aid that heals our sadness. It's the paint brush that vibrantly colors our life."

Mindi Davis, Writer, intuitive, wife, mother

69

"Okay, so first I should let you know that I'm a certified Laughter Yoga Leader (laughteryoga.org), which tells you I love laughter and the effect it has on me and on the people I work with.

The website I mentioned has lots of information about laughter. So does laughteryogaamerica.com. There are so many types of laughter: the laughter of self-consciousness, the laughter of appreciation, the laughter of surprise, the laughter to cover fear or embarrassment, the laughter of delight, uncontrollable gleeful laughter, nasty and sarcastic laughter, intellectually amused laughter and the laughter of connection. The list goes on and on.

Genuine, spontaneous laughter seems to be a form of emotional expression and connection, a way to release energy.

The types of laughter I enjoy the most are:

When there is a shift from left brain linear logic into right brain creativity and playfulness. When silliness and a sense of the absurd can reign and inhibitions and fears dissolve into giggles. This is when the ego steps aside and we take ourselves and life lightly. I often experience this type in Laughter Yoga sessions.

When I've laughed with sheer delight at a stupendously beautiful sunset, or while spinning on a dance floor.

When it comes bubbling up and out of inner joy as a result of a deep connection or shared experience/awareness.

When I play improvised music with a group of people, and sometimes after we've come to the end of a particularly wonderful piece, we just start laughing.

I think about the Dalai Lama, who has been through so much hardship, yet often laughs so genuinely. One thing Laughter Yoga taught me is that an inner resource is always available.

Brother Stendl-Rast said something like it isn't happiness that makes us laugh, we are happy because we laugh. Laughter is a choice, as in I can choose to respond to my computer messing up with curses or laughter. I can choose to respond to the traffic jam with frustration or amused laughter."

Peggy Tileston, MA, MT-BC, CMS, CLYL,
Wellness therapist and educator

"Laughter is medicine for the soul.

It's a way to not take things too seriously. When you make mistakes, laughing about it lifts the burden of dwelling on it.

It can be a way to forgive yourself and move on. Children are quick to laugh because they're not too weighed down with other considerations. They find joy in simple things. Adults could benefit by being less serious and more willing to chuckle or enjoy a good laugh.

In our family, playing games can bring out so much laughter that tears begin to flow.

Everyone feels better after a good laughfest."

Pete Codella, Digital public relations counselor

"You feel it in your mind, it bubbles down to your stomach and it massages everything along the way."

Mary Ann Gogoleski, Director/Founder, Agoraphobics In Motion

"Laughter is spending time with my three daughters and their families from all over the USA, from Ohio to Florida. I have three grandsons and two granddaughters, whom I love dearly."

Rhea Steele McCoy, Housewife

"Laughter is ancient and primeval — emerging from the darkest and deepest forbidding canyons in the soul. Laughter is an enigma of the highest order; unleashed and unbridled to the winds in full stride it is, at its core essence, deliciously untamed and unstable, springing forth from uncharted storehouses. The twin torrents of childhood joy and grown-up grief converge synergistically in a spontaneous combustion of uninterrupted and melodious soundscapes, copiously filling the silence of the void of our deepest longing."

Rick Schuler, Singer, songwriter

74

"A funny thing, laughter is. (No pun intended.)

It's something that can't be controlled, and no matter how much we try to stifle a laugh it can stay with us long after whatever we thought was funny becomes a thing of the past.

There have been times when I could be performing the most mundane task when a random thought suddenly pops up in my brain. It either stimulates a chuckle, or a hearty laugh — one that can take minutes to stop or in an instant can turn into tears.

I love hearing other people laugh. I also enjoy the variety of sounds that emanate from different people. I enjoy hearty, loud and unrestrained laughter — the type that allows one to let loose and fill us with a rush of adrenaline, accompanied by a physical change that others notice: red cheeks, tears, deep breathing and release.

Then there's the type of laughter that can be sarcastic, rude and downright wicked. I sometimes refer to it as LOL laughter.

Whatever anyone thinks or says, I believe laughter soothes the soul."

Raquel Algarin, Non-profit executive director

"Laughter is the gift of personal joy when prompted by another joyous occurrence from any of the senses — tactile, auditory, visual, olfactory and taste. It comes as a beautiful natural response, be it the giver or the receiver."

Rob Melton, Painter

"I once saw a quote that summed it up: 'Laughter is as intimate as you can get without touching someone.' I believe this is true. It isn't just an action, but a feeling — a way of life.

When I laugh with the ones I love it brings me more into the moment. I feel love and energy from all the people I'm with. This is especially true with my soulmate, Flora. In fact, when getting to know each other I would say about 40 percent of our time spent together involved laughter, which of course brought us even closer. Laughter is healthy.

If you don't laugh then you aren't living. You're simply going through the motions of existing."

Rene Harris, Filmmaker

"Laughter may be the best medicine, but sometimes just taking the right 'medicine' can make things seem a lot funnier.

Laughter is contagious. If we had a national 'Laugh Out Loud Day,' I wonder how long it would take to bring peace to the Middle East.

I bet that if someone really laughed their butt off, they wouldn't think it was so funny.

It may be true that he who laughs last, laughs best. But I believe that he who laughs most often, especially with those he loves, will be happier and more content in the long run."

Doug Weiser, Filmmaker, firefighter

"I believe we are all born with the seed of joy in our hearts.

I equate laughter with that tickle that lives inside of us, and honor it as one of our great gifts to be nurtured and savored throughout our lifetime.

Laughter heals the body, connects us to others and aligns us to spirit.

It's the precious alchemy for a happy life."

Goldie Hawn, Actress, director, producer

"Laughter is second only to Love.

It warms the soul from the inside out and by the time it reaches the surface, it becomes deliciously contagious.

Who can watch someone giggling with absolute glee and not join them in their merriment? At a very young age, my darling granddad, George Bowers, taught me one of my life's most important lessons. He said: 'When you look back at life, no matter how dire the situation was that you experienced in the past, you will be able to find humor in it. Time makes it so.'

But you don't need time. The trick is to be able to sit in any difficult situation and find the humor. It's in you. You just have to look for it."

Pinsie Perkins, IT manager

"Laughter is being able to get through the day. I lost my oldest child five years ago. He was 24. I found that if I learned to laugh again I could go on.

We should have a joyful heart when we worship God. Laughter gives me that.

I find that I enjoy making others laugh because they, too, may have a broken heart that needs healing. With God, faith, love, laughter and friends in your life, you can get up and face the world."

Rhonda Ducroz, Waitress

"Laughter is gratitude. Laughter is the body's way of saying, 'Thank you!' Thanks for making me feel alive. Thanks for unleashing my brain. Thanks for uncorking my body. And thank you, laughter, for your infectious nature to bring out this feeling in others to share in our mirth.

And that's just the physical part.

On a metaphysical level, uncontrollable laughter relieves stress, social tension, creates connections and reinforces bonds between people. The ability to laugh at yourself is spiritual maturity.

Hilarity leads to clarity."

Ruth Weisberg, Radio host

"Laughter is the sound of your soul releasing its gratitude."

Ralph Castro, Retired

"When my niece, who is about eight, sits on my lap, sees a winged ant sitting on my arm and then suddenly pipes up with 'These ants have wings so they can do their jobs.'

I just crack up there and then. You can imagine what thoughts went through my head."

Ruth Lennie, Scientist

"Laughter is warmth.

Laughter is a moment in time when your insides feel so good and your body vibrates with an intense feeling of well-being. To be in a room when someone makes a joke or some silly thing happens and everyone starts to chuckle at once. It's a wonderful joy to be part of. The laughter is so overwhelming that you can't control it. Everyone holds their sides as if the explosion of the moment could pull you apart.

I love those times — when the laugher is so strong and impossible to control. Laughter makes things better. It helps heal anger and hurts. Laughter bathes you in happiness, even if it's just for a minute or two."

Rikki Karn, Physician assistant

⟡

"For me, laughter is an extension of self.

For as long as I can remember I have enjoyed the freedom of release that laughter gives. When I was a child and became tickled by a situation I would sometimes laugh so deeply that my knees would become weak. I'd fall to the floor and roll around in fits of laughter.

Laughter is a great stress reliever. It brings a rush of cleansing air into the lungs and sometimes when exhaled can take away loads of frustration and sadness.

Laughter is a big part of who I am."

Sabreen Ameen, Unfortunately, still unemployed

"Laughter is my life. I'm an actor, singer and dancer. Every part I get usually has something to do with my love of laughter.

My cats were named after two characters in *The Lucy Show*, Fred and Ethel, because they made me laugh.

The silliest little things make me laugh. I even laugh at bad jokes. What is laughter? It's me. It's even my e-mail address: hotlaughs@aol.com."

Sharon Geller, Actress, humorist, teacher

83

"Laughter is life's medicine. The harder life gets the more I crave those joyous moments and gatherings with my friends, whether it's real time or online. There's nothing like a good ol' LOL to make your day just a little bit better.

There have been seasons of sadness in my life. During those days I would grab a blanket, curl up on the couch and just let the latest Seinfeld marathon work its magic. When worries drag me down, nobody chases those blues away like Comedy Central's Stephen Colbert, with a wag of his finger or a Threat Level alert for America. (I do believe bears are the number-one threat facing America.)

I can't remember a time when laughter didn't carry me to a better place. It's the very essence of pure joy wrapped in one big, loud guffaw."

Roxanne Torre, Domestic engineer

"The Sufis say that unless you can laugh easily and often, you have no soul.

For me, laughter exists in those moments of incongruity; those flashes of binding where new meaning takes shape. That, and Moe hitting Curly on the head with a hammer, because I believe all humor is based on pain in some way.

The other day I was arguing with my son and I said, 'You know, someday you'll have children of your own.' And he said, 'Yeah. Someday so may you.' There is absolutely nothing funny about this, except the incongruity between expectation and meaning, the surprise of frustrated expectation.

Laughter creates new insights, new meaning. It ameliorates our pain and spiritualizes our souls."

Scott McPartland, Tour guide, college professor

"Laughter is a rainbow for the heart."

Stephanie L. Worrall, Legal research editor

"One way to look at laughter would be Eugene Ionesco's in *The Bald Soprano*. Two things which are normal in themselves but become absurd when juxtaposed: Two people who ask everyday questions like what's your name and where do you live — and find that they are married and living in the same house.

Neither a man walking on the street nor a banana is funny but put together it makes for slapstick humor. Laughter restores balance. It helps us see how ridiculous we are when we take ourselves seriously. Laughter is Santa's merry Ho, Ho, Ho in the midst of the darkest winter. It's accepting life, warts and all, and accepting how small and silly and gorgeous we can be when we distance ourselves from our egos."

Dr. Pramila Davidson, Retired professor

"What better way to bounce back from the indignities, vanities and failures that are all a part of the human experience than to have the capacity to laugh?   We can all identify with the observation by calligrapher Jennifer Vane: 'I try to take one day at a time, but sometimes several days attack me at once.'

One of my friends loves to say, 'I try to judge any experience in terms of its future anecdotal value.' What a wonderful philosophy of life — and a powerful antidote to the feelings of dismay and despair that try to creep into our lives on occasion.

I like to think of laughter as visible evidence that a sense of humor is a gift from the Divine."

Sharon Turnbull, Chief inspiration officer and webmistress of www.GoddessGift.com

"The urge to laugh can be an expression of emotions in a situation that isn't funny. It's the release valve on a pressure cooker. Sometimes it's used as an expression of agreement.

How many times have you laughed when a friend leaves and says, 'See you later?' Was that funny? Were you that happy to see them go?

I believe laughter is the human expression of many emotions — and not necessarily that of joy or happiness."

Sonya Johnson, Accounting

"I am an educator at a community college in Ontario. When my Chair audited my class her first comment was that of all the classes she had visited, mine was the only one in which students laughed.

I take that as a good sign. My sections are filled before most other sections. Students report that they would rather wait two years to get into my classes instead of selecting another teacher.

Students think I'm friendly and approachable. I think it's because I don't hesitate to smile and laugh.

Laughter is contagious. It even reaches students who appear shy and stay to themselves in a back corner of the classroom. Laughter makes people wonder what we're up to.

As people pass our classroom they become 'rubber-neckers' — peering and peeking, trying to see what is going on. Sometimes people just stop at the door and look into the classroom with a dumbfounded expression on their faces.

My students learn an important theory. They say the process is easier because they have fun and are free to laugh. Attendance isn't an issue in my classroom. Students say they feel good and look forward to the class as the highlight of their entire week.

I've heard laughter called a 'social lubricant' and I agree. Laughter cuts tension and makes us feel good. It makes us feel closer to one another, and that heightens the trust level. Students are more apt to share personal issues. We never laugh at each other or our issues, but we do laugh with each other.

One of the classes where students have great fun is when we learn about Dr. Kataria and practice Laughter Yoga. I assign 'Wacky Homework of the Week.' Two examples are: Teach someone Laughter Yoga. Smile to reduce free-floating hostility.

Laughter takes the seriousness out of being a student. Students face so much stress with conflicting roles: parenting, bread-winning, being employed and more. There are financial and situational pressures. Many students are new to the country and laughter helps them feel relaxed as they laugh away some of the stress chemicals that build up inside their bodies.

I experience arthritis symptoms which can make mobility and functioning a real challenge some days. When I have arthritic flares on days that I teach, I find that I leave the classroom feeling much better than I did before I arrived. We're often laughing while I'm teaching. I'm completely unaware of my pain."

Shirley Wood, Wellness/stress management educator

"Laughter is a gift from God and our primate ancestors.

It can be gentle or powerful. It jump-starts our circulation, our breathing and our immune system. It surprises us with its spontaneity.

It reminds us we are alive."

Steven E. Hodes, Gastroenterologist, metaphysician

"Laughter is when you color your hair a lighter shade, admire the highlights and then realize there are silver hairs the new color didn't cover."

Shelley Birch, Retired

"I grew up around people who were Irish, Italian and Hispanic. They were social drinkers who liked to mingle. I lived in bars and was constantly around people who used humor to get through the day.

It didn't matter if the situation was good or bad. There was always a joke to be told and a shoulder to be patted.

Humor, to me, is taking real-life issues, described in a funny way, to pass a moment of anxiety.

Life is too short to be sad. Laughter starts deep within the core, touching our heart and eyes and makes us friendlier to others, opening doors to friendships.

I'm always looking for a funny joke to post on Facebook — especiallly when I'm depressed."

Susan Mahoney, Works with the homeless

"Laughter is a release of joy. It has been proven to be beneficial to your health, and feels wonderful at the moment.

It's contagious. It tends to make others smile and laugh with you. It's Prozac without the side effects."

Sue Pompetti, Self-employed

"Laughter is the tool that makes sure I don't take myself or my world too seriously.

The ability to see the absurdity in most situations keeps me sane. It keeps my sense of balance. Besides, the physical act of laughing — a good belly laugh, that is — boosts the immune system and makes other people smile.

What could be better?"

Susan Alexander, Fundraiser

"Laughter is a God-given response that shows happiness, fright and uneasiness. In each case, laughter makes the soul brighter by releasing a chemical that elevates the sensation of happiness.

Laughter is a gift that shouldn't be wasted, but cherished and spread as often as possible to everyone, and not just those who are special.

Susan Cooler, Adjunct instructor

"Laughter is warm. Laughter is light. And it works day and night."

Taria Cavell-Chesterman, Photographer, therapist, entertainer

"Laughter is a snicker, a giggle, a chuckle, or a fall out of your seat. Oh my God! There are tears rolling down my face and I can't stop. It's an emotional experience!

These experiences can be brought on by something absurd, goofy, silly, humorous, ludicrous or hysterical. It's an emotion we should all enjoy experiencing more of."

Vivianne Trueba, Community liaison

"When I was in my forties, I committed to laughing an hour a day for a year as part of my spiritual process.

The first two laughs were like a bad joke—forced and flat. By the third laugh, the absurdity of the first two wacky attempts fired my sense of humor into an effervescent laughter, perceived as drinking golden joy through every bodily cell.

During this year-long focus on laughter, a friend living far away in Alaska called. Once she announced who she was, happiness triggered my laughter. For the next 45 minutes both of us laughed. Any attempts at words only catapulted the laughter to the next level of more and more giggles, tears, inability to contain such joy other than sharing it. An ecstatic high based solely on laughter.

Since then, regardless of what life manifests — difficulty or pleasure — my access to the joy of laughter has remained an eager treasure trove.

I am so grateful in my life's journey I gave myself time to mature laughter as an art, a divinity and an articulation of joy."

Tanai Starrs, Spiritual healer, visionary

"Laughter is the most joyous thing in the world, the bubbling over of happiness when something strikes you as really, really funny.

When you laugh at something in the company of others it brings a wonderful feeling of unity. The walls between people dissolve and your spirits soar together.

Fortunately, I think my husband is unbelievably funny — his quick wit has kept me laughing and helped me through difficult times for over 40 years."

Wendy Schuman, Freelance editor and writer

"Laughter is joy's cousin and grief's worst enemy.

I remember being so sad and depressed after my father unexpectedly died just a few months after my wedding. He was diagnosed with mad cow disease, and I watched painfully as it ravaged his body and mind in a matter of months.

My father had many wonderful traits, but one of his best was that he loved to laugh. As a grade school principal, he was always surrounded by children who were overflowing with laughter. As a legacy to my father, I decided that I needed to start finding more laughter in the world.

My business partner, an artist, and I decided to start creating humorous sayings and illustrations for women and called them 'Working Girls.' We just knew it felt good to laugh and create humor. We never really realized that it would have such commercial success. Today, there are over 500 products with Working Girl sayings on them — everything from pajamas and keychains to paper plates, napkins and calendars.

To me, laughter is life. It's living. Laughter is the best way to honor those we've loved and lost."

Tonja Steel, Owner, Working Girls brand

"One thing that is irresistible to me is a man who can make me laugh. I find it very sexy."

Rachelle Pachtman, PR consultant

"Laughter is the best medicine, as the old expression goes.

Laughter can stop an argument in its tracks. Laughter can exercise your innards and make you laugh until it hurts.

Laughter can make friends out of total strangers. Laughter is one of the best things to share. Laughter is the sound that happiness makes."

Susan Hamilton, Sales clerk, jewelry artist

"Laughter, real laughter, is like a deep massage from the inside out.

It's a delicious strain on my muscles. It pushes them to open to accept more joy in my body and my life.

Laughter is an expansion, a stretch. It brings us into the realm of allowing our highest purpose: joy."

Valerie Reiss, Writer

"Laughter is that capacity for joy that springs within us at unexpected moments.

It pokes fun at the world and at people. It works on the body like a yoga session and like Kriya breathing. It lifts the world off the shoulders and creates a sense of unity in a group — effortlessly.

It's a hidden necessity in life. It keeps the ego in check. Shared humor can keep a marriage together. It keeps friends with you. A skillful comedian can reflect the world back to you and make you laugh at it or with it. It sometimes seems like the ultimate understanding of the world and sometimes, one's place in it."

Veryan Edwards, Artist

Laughing along...

With Bill Clinton

With Glenn Campbell

With The Dalai Lama

With Jim Nabors

With John Denver

With Goldie Hawn

With Richard Gere

With Tibetan Buddhist Monks

With Dick Clark

With Jimmy Carter

With Prince Charles

With Prince William

With Roy Rogers

With Totie Fields

With The Big Bad Wolf

With Marty Allen

With Romero Britto

105

LEXIE BROCKWAY POTAMKIN

Lexie Brockway Potamkin brings a diverse career and extensive world travel to her work as author of *What is Spirit?; What is Peace?; What is Love?; What is Death?*, and now *What is Laughter?*. A human rights activist, counselor and minister, she spent many years working in the world of business, entertainment and media. A former Miss World USA, she hosted her own talk show and eventually became a public relations professional working for Golin Harris Public Relations, Gold Mills, Inc., and Rogers and Cowan Public Relations. At the height of her success in business, having founded and sold her own PR firm, she returned to school for her master's degree in applied psychology from the University of Santa Monica. Her ensuing counseling work inspired her to take the next spiritual step, becoming an ordained minister.

Lexie has traveled the world and over the past decade has been a guiding force and inspiration for many charitable organizations. She and her husband founded an elementary school in Fisher Island, Florida. Lexie serves on various non-profit boards, teaches meditation classes and she believes that giving and receiving are the same. The more you give, the more you receive.

Lexie is the mother of three children and writes inspirational books for adults.

ROMERO BRITTO

Romero Britto is a Brazilian artist based in Miami, Florida. Born in the disadvantaged area of Recife, he taught himself at an early age by painting on surfaces such as newspapers.

In 1983, he traveled to Paris, where he was introduced to the work of Matisse and Picasso. He combined influences from cubism with pop to create a vibrant and iconic style that, as *The New York Times* described, "exudes warmth, optimism and love." In 1998, Britto relocated to Miami and emerged as an international artist. His work was selected alongside Andy Warhol and Keith Haring's for Absolut Vodka's "Absolut Art" campaign.

Britto's artwork has since been exhibited in galleries and museums in over 100 countries, including the Salon Nationale des Beaux-Arts exhibition at the Carrousel du Louvre in Paris, the Museum of Contemporary Art in Shanghai, Museu da Imagem e do Som in Sao Paulo, Brazil.

His work can also be found in the collection of the California Museum of Art Oakland, the Miami Children's Museum and numerous private collections. He has also created public art installations for the O2 Dome (Berlin), Hyde Park, (London), John F. Kennedy Airport (New York) and Cirque du Soleil at Super Bowl XLI.

His colorful children's books and calendars have been published by Simon & Shuster and Rizzoli.

Try This at Home
Bring More Laughter into Your Home

My brother-in-law, Alan, is a skilled joke teller, and he brings so much joy to others with his humor. He showed me a way to get my children out of the house and off to school without being so serious or feeling the pressures of the morning rush. He makes them laugh!

While staying with us during a school week, he would get up in the morning and send the kids off with jokes. He came up with really funny stuff, often searching online for material at the crack of dawn. I saw my kids becoming so much happier in the morning because of this morning joke ritual.

Here are some ways to make yourself, your friends and your children laugh:

1. Create a daily laughter ritual
Whether it's a round of tickling or sharing a funny story, come up with something you can share with your children every day at a special time. Morning, dinnertime or bedtime.

2. Post funny jokes

When you find jokes you really, really like, spread them around the house. Put them on Post-it notes in places your family frequents, and give them a good laugh.

3. Leave funny messages

Since most of our children have cell phones, call or text a

funny joke or message during school hours that will bring a smile when they listen or see it on the way home.

4. Sing a silly song

Don't worry about embarrassing yourself. When you're willing to be funny and silly, your kids will seem as if they are being entertained by a star the likes of Jennifer Lopez or Justin Bieber.

5. Send a note to school

A way to your child's funny bone may be through leaving a funny note in his or her lunch box — something that cracks them up when they pull out their sandwich and juice.

6. Keep goofy jokes handy

Keep funny jokes in your pocket, and write new ones if you can. Have jokes ready for times of crankiness and boredom. They're great for road trips, too.

7. Funny animals with messages

Get a stuffed animal your child will love and attach a funny message or private joke only your child will chuckle over.

8. Get inspired by movies and songs

When you hear a line that makes you laugh, write it down and add it to your arsenal of funny messages. Use the line as needed for cheering, healing and to inspire laughing out loud.

9. Watch funny TV and movies

Nothing is more fun than watching a hilarious movie or TV show. Identify the favorites that work every time and keep them on hand for viewing pleasure. Laugh, laugh, laugh.

10. Call a friend with a great sense of humor

Sharing a laugh is all you need to get through the day.

Inspirational Sources

The Origins of Laughter, by Dr. John Morreall

Marina Davila-Ross, from University of Portsmouth, England

Robert Provine, Neurobiologist

Anatomy of an Illness, Norman Cousins

Dr. Michael Miller and Dr. William Fry, University of Maryland Medical Center

Jiten Kohi, Founder and President, Hasya Yoga Kendra. Chairman, Institute of Laughter Yoga, India

Laugh for no Reason, by Dr. Madan Kataria

My Spiritual Journey, by The Dalai Lama

INDEX